When the Slave Esperança Garcia Wrote a Letter

Groundwood Books / House of Anansi Press
110 Spadina Avenue, Suite 801, Toronto, Ontario M5V 2K4
or c/o Publishers Group West
1700 Fourth Street, Berkeley, CA 94710

Note: The language in Esperança Garcia's letter has been adapted
for contemporary readers.

We acknowledge for their financial support of our publishing program the
Government of Canada through the Canada Book Fund (CBF).

Library and Archives Canada Cataloguing in Publication
Rosa, Sonia
[Quando a escrava Esperança Garcia escreveu uma carta. English]
When the slave Esperança Garcia wrote a letter /
written by Sonia Rosa ; illustrated by Luciana Justiniani Hees ;
translated by Jane Springer.

Translation of: Quando a escrava Esperança Garcia escreveu uma carta.
Issued in print and electronic formats.
ISBN 978-1-55498-729-0 (bound).—ISBN 978-1-55498-730-6 (html)

I. Springer, Jane, translator II. Hees, Luciana Justiniani, illustrator
III. Title. IV. Title: Quando a escrava Esperança Garcia escreveu uma
carta. English

PZ7.R687Wh 2015   j869.3'5   C2015-900108-0
C2015-900109-9

The illustrations were drawn in pencil and colored digitally; brush-painted elements
were scanned and incorporated digitally.
Printed and bound in Malaysia

When the Slave Esperança Garcia Wrote a Letter

Written by Sonia Rosa

Illustrated by Luciana Justiniani Hees

Translated by Jane Springer

Groundwood Books
House of Anansi Press
Toronto Berkeley

This book is dedicated to the memory of my mother,
Adir Rosa de Oliveira, and my aunt, Arlinda Rosa Ferreira —
the most important women in my life —
who taught me how to live, to fight, to love and to dream.

Esperança Garcia is famous in the Brazilian state of Piauí, and I would like her to be celebrated all over Brazil and the rest of the world. The memory of this woman, like hope for a better life, can never die.

My name is Esperança Garcia.

Everybody has a story, and so do I.

I am a slave, married, with children. I used to live with my family in Fazenda dos Algodões — a cotton farm. My owners were Jesuit priests.

After the priests had to return to Europe, my life got much worse.

I can't lie. The priests did not treat my family so badly. I learned a lot from them — most important, how to read and write. I became an educated slave. I was lucky. Where I am now, very few women know how to read. It's even worse for women slaves — most can't even recognize their own names.

Yet I can't say I was happy, because for a slave, a happy life isn't possible.

Now, against my wishes, I have a very different life. I was forced to leave Fazenda dos Algodões to work as a cook at the home of Captain Antonio Vieira de Couto.

I have been separated from my husband, and I miss him terribly. I have always worked without rest, but now I can't hug my husband and my children every day. My family was divided up. My husband has the older children on the farm, and I came here with the two younger ones.

As if the sorrow of separation isn't enough, now I have to put up with the captain's blows. I can't understand why this new master beats people so much.

But my most precious joy is reading and writing. It is a way of expanding a person and allowing their voice to spread to places far away, places never imagined …

Learning to read and write has helped me understand the world and has made me angry about the injustices and horrors of slavery.

I, Esperança Garcia, woman, mother and slave, have decided to write a letter to the governor to tell him about my suffering, my anger and my wish for change. I am not ashamed to ask for his help after the sudden separation of my family and all the mistreatment my little children and I are going through. Others who came with me to the captain's house are also being badly treated. The captain seems to have a stone in place of a heart.

The priests taught me their religion and so all my children have been baptized, except for the youngest one. It's been a long time since I went to confession or mass, and I still need to baptize my daughter. I want to return to Fazenda dos Algodões as soon as possible.

My fingers, worn out from so much work, pick up the pen to write this letter. In it I tell the governor everything, every little detail. He's the only one who can solve my problem and bring my family back together.

I have a copy of the letter that I keep safe, close to me.

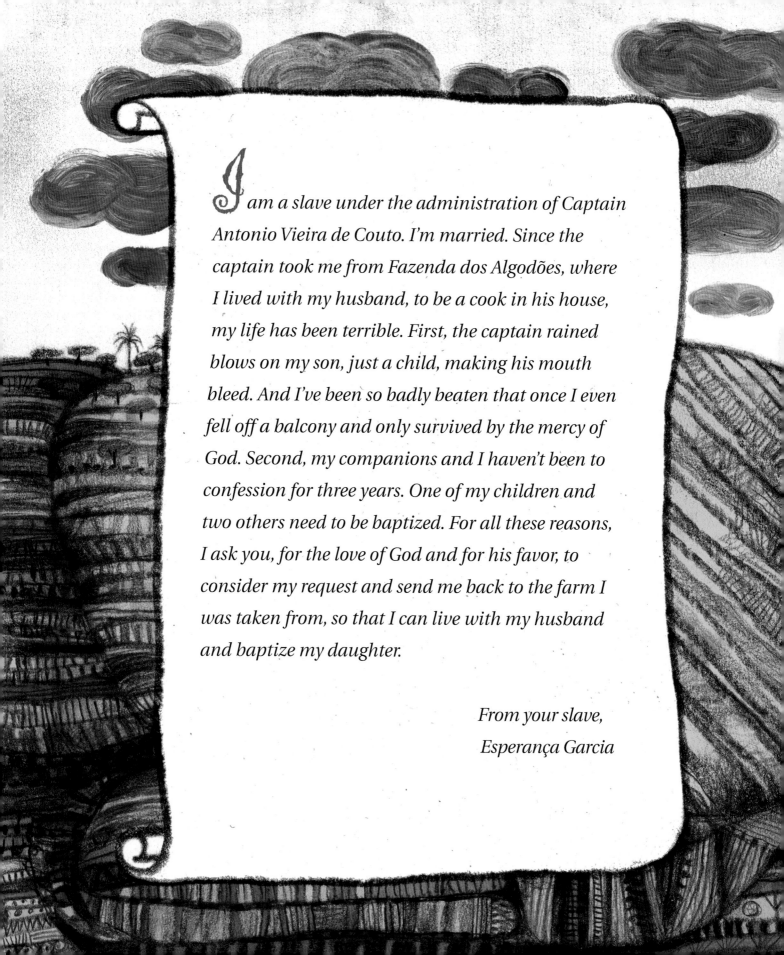

I am a slave under the administration of Captain Antonio Vieira de Couto. I'm married. Since the captain took me from Fazenda dos Algodões, where I lived with my husband, to be a cook in his house, my life has been terrible. First, the captain rained blows on my son, just a child, making his mouth bleed. And I've been so badly beaten that once I even fell off a balcony and only survived by the mercy of God. Second, my companions and I haven't been to confession for three years. One of my children and two others need to be baptized. For all these reasons, I ask you, for the love of God and for his favor, to consider my request and send me back to the farm I was taken from, so that I can live with my husband and baptize my daughter.

From your slave,
Esperança Garcia

*T*oday, after another day of hard work in the kitchen, I'm comforted when my little children wrap themselves around my legs. I'm still waiting for an answer to the letter I sent to the governor. It seems it will never arrive.

Meanwhile I carry on, living the life that I can…

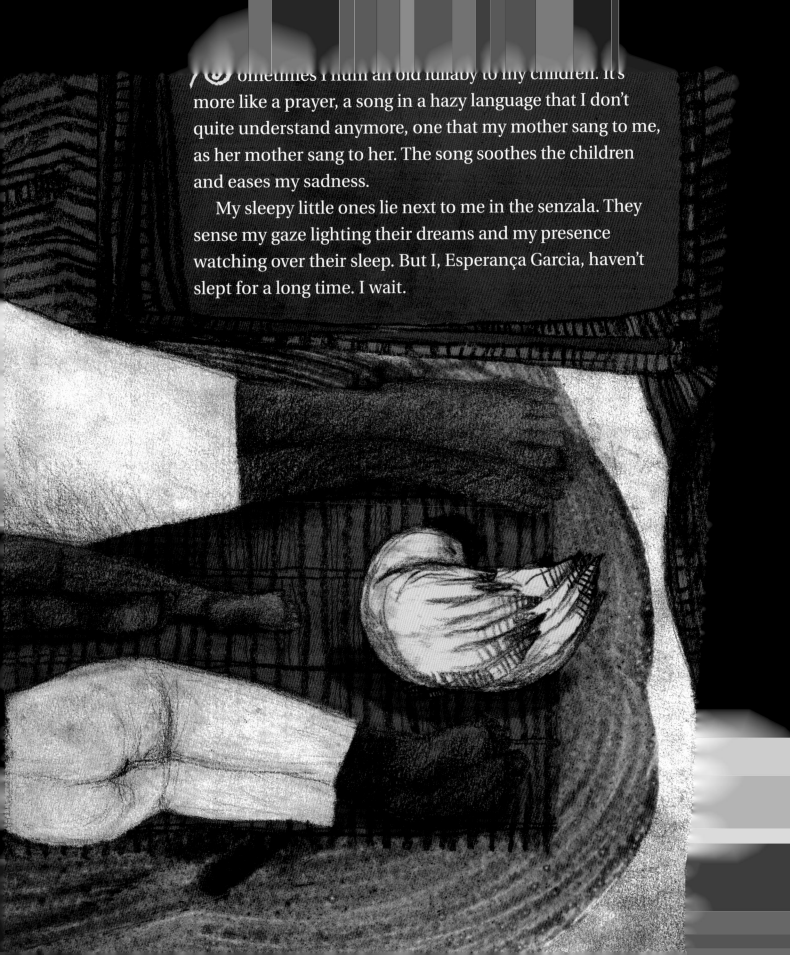

Sometimes I hum an old lullaby to my children. It's more like a prayer, a song in a hazy language that I don't quite understand anymore, one that my mother sang to me, as her mother sang to her. The song soothes the children and eases my sadness.

My sleepy little ones lie next to me in the senzala. They sense my gaze lighting their dreams and my presence watching over their sleep. But I, Esperança Garcia, haven't slept for a long time. I wait.

Today another day has passed
without news…
   Who knows if tomorrow I'll have
a surprise?

Morning came softly. A timid sun graced the sky. Birds were singing in the trees.

It was time for Esperança Garcia to get up. She rose from another sleepless night. She slowly fixed her hair and wiped away the tears that kept falling, even as she struggled to hold them back. Today was another day of waiting for the answer to her letter.

A little later, as she was preparing breakfast for her master, Esperança Garcia could think of nothing else. The answer could arrive at any moment.

$\mathcal{L}$ater, at lunchtime, the busiest time of the day, her cheeks began to drip from the heat of the wood stove. Her warm tears fell, mingling with the sweat on her face.

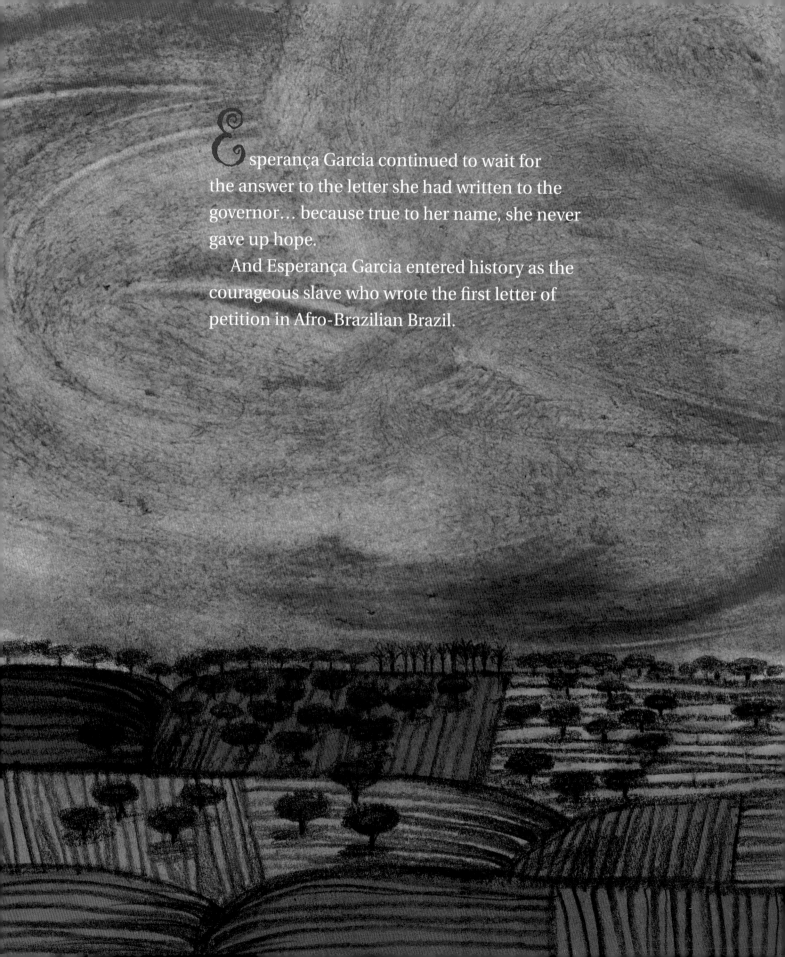

Esperança Garcia continued to wait for the answer to the letter she had written to the governor… because true to her name, she never gave up hope.

And Esperança Garcia entered history as the courageous slave who wrote the first letter of petition in Afro-Brazilian Brazil.

Esperança Garcia's voice was a forceful cry for liberation, and it has not been in vain. She is truly an unforgettable woman!

Historical Notes

As a slave on a farm run by Jesuit priests, Esperança Garcia most certainly learned to read and write and was baptized and confirmed in the Catholic faith. Her name, which means hope, must have been given to her by the priests. The Jesuits were expelled from Portugal and its colonies by the Marquês de Pombal in the mid-eighteenth century.

We don't know where or when
Esperança Garcia was born. However, she
showed remarkable courage in writing
the first letter of petition to a governor
complaining about her mistreatment by
Captain Antonio Vieira de Couto, inspector
of Nazaré, now a city in Piauí state.

Esperança Garcia's letter is dated
September 6, 1770, and is addressed
to the governor of Maranhão, Gonçalo
Lourenço Botelho de Castro. At that time
Maranhão and Piauí were part of the same
administrative division.

We don't know if she ever received a
reply.

Atlantic Ocean

São Luis
do Maranhão

MARANHÃO

Fazenda dos Algodões

Fazenda do Captain
Antonio Vieira de Couto

PIAUÍ

N
W   E
S

Following historian Luiz Mott's discovery of a copy of the letter in the public archives of Piauí in 1979, September 6 became Black Consciousness Day in the state. Schools and cultural groups in Teresina, the capital of Piauí, are now named after Esperança Garcia.

The original letter is archived in Lisbon, Portugal, and is part of the record of Brazilian colonial history.

Sonia Rosa was born and lives in Rio de Janeiro. She is a teacher with a specialty in reading, culture and African history. She has written more than thirty-five books, and her work has been recognized by the Brazilian chapter of the International Board on Books for Young People (FNLIJ) and the White Ravens Catalogue.

Luciana Justiniani Hees is a Brazilian illustrator who lived in Mozambique for many years and now lives in Oporto, Portugal. She has illustrated a number of books with African and Afro-Brazilian themes. An exhibition of her work was held at the Franco-Mozam-bican Cultural Center in Maputo, and her short film *O Salão Azul* was selected for the International Film Festival in Rotterdam.

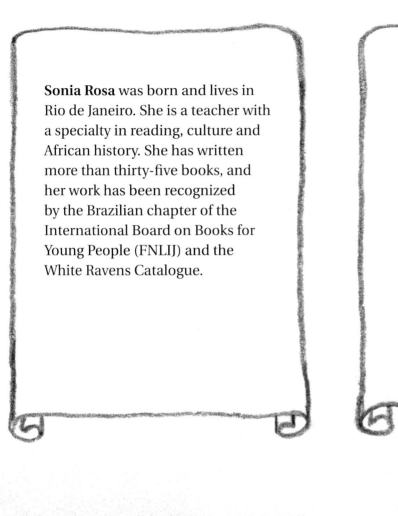